The Big Ideas Club Presents

Living Myths
Visual Philosophy

The Illustrated Nietzsche:
Zarathustra Descended and Spoke

Book III:
The Laughing Ascent and the Shadows We Shed

A Visual Companion to Nietzsche's Zarathustra

By Jason Kassel, PhD
© 2025
Recursive Publishing

Table of Contents

⛰ Introduction to Book III

When the Flame Returns

Zarathustra had gone into silence.

Not out of weakness. Not out of defeat. But because the world was not ready—and neither was he.

Now, he returns. But he does not return unchanged.

This is not the voice of the mountain.
 This is the voice of one who has seen the abyss inside and below.
 This is not a teacher's return.
 It is a flame that comes to test what still stands.

In Book III, the laughter deepens.
 It is no longer mockery or defiance—it is creation.
 The crowd remains faceless.
 But the philosopher?
 He becomes stranger, freer, more terrifying.

He speaks in riddles.
 He leaves when they begin to understand.
 He plants seeds in ruin.
 He listens only to the silence that has learned how to sing.

Book III does not resolve anything.
It opens the possibility that resolution is the wrong goal.

You will not follow Zarathustra.
You will watch him vanish.

And in that vanishing, something inside you may begin to take shape.

How to Read This Book

(When Meaning Refuses to Explain Itself)

This is not a chapter book.

This is not a narrative.

This is not philosophy explained.

It is fifteen symbolic modules—each a scene, an image, a silence.

Each one includes:

1. Mythic Image

    A symbolic moment drawn from *Thus Spoke Zarathustra*.

2. Nietzsche's Aphorism

    A paraphrased fragment from the original German—compressed, sharp, or silent.

3. 🔍 Image Prompt

    Find the hidden patterns, break the assumed logic.

4. AI-Literacy Challenges

    Let artificial intelligence help you invert and reimagine meaning.

5. 🔖 Reflective + Creative Tasks

Draw, name, reverse, or reshape the myth. Not for grades—for growth.

6. 🎭 The Anonymous Mask

Look for the unnamed figures.
Ask who is absent—and why you're still watching.

This is not a book to be mastered.
It is a book to interrupt your assumptions.

You will not leave this book with answers.
You will leave it with new questions shaped like mirrors.

Read slowly.
Return often.
Skip freely.

And when you laugh—not because it is funny, but because it is true—you will know:
Book III has begun.

□□ Chapter 1: The Spiral Path

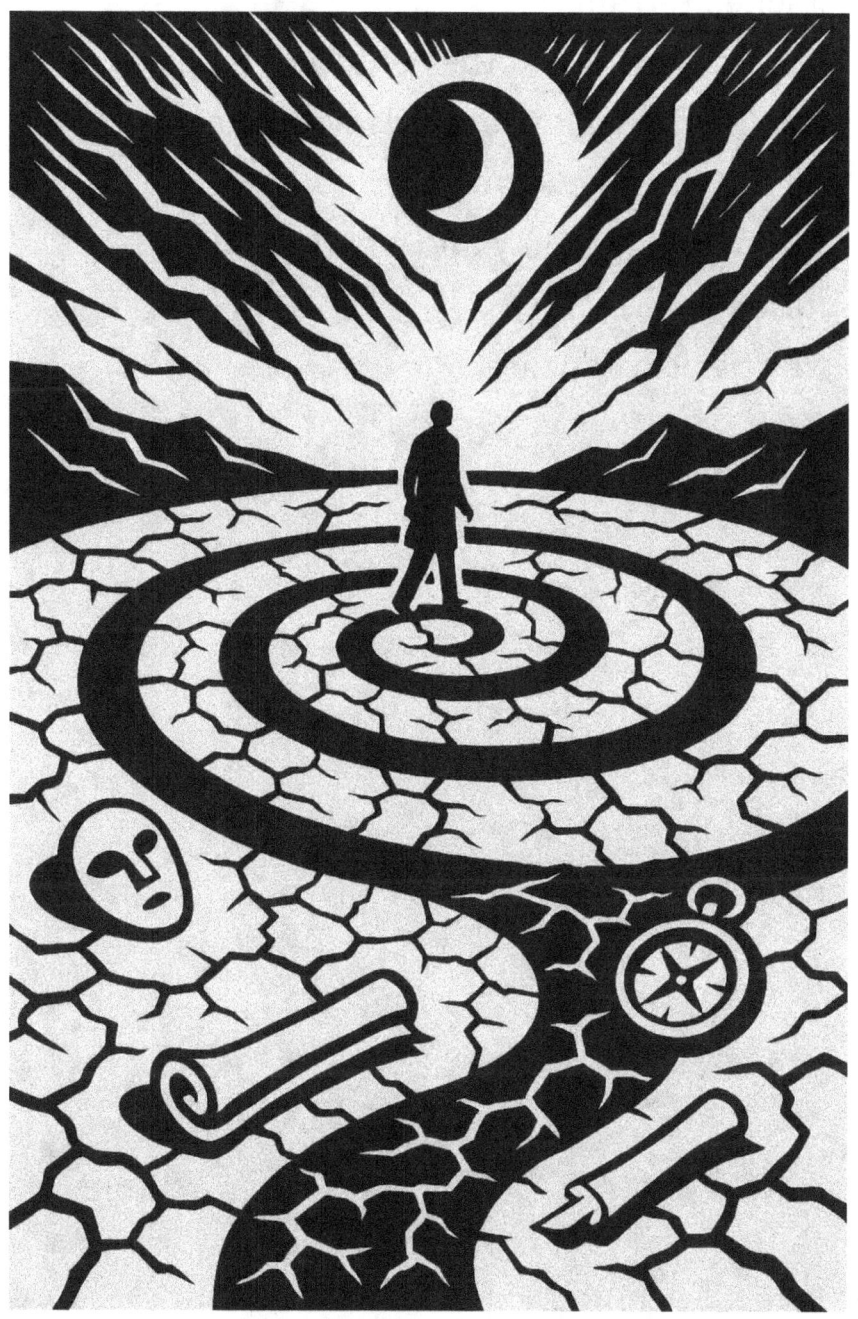

□ Image & Scene Summary

A solitary figure walks a spiral path carved into cracked terrain.

The figure is not at the center—but near it.

Around the spiral: discarded objects—a mask, a scroll, a broken compass.

Above: a jagged sky and a half-shaded crescent sun.

No one else appears.

◣ How It Works

Diagram Name: *The Geometry of Becoming*

- Spiral = not repetition, but deepening

- Outer ring = inherited roles, beliefs, distractions (mask, scroll, compass)

- Inner movement = personal meaning gained through cyclical return

- Sun = partial clarity—vision still unfolding
  Mechanism:

The spiral teaches: not all progress is forward. Some paths must circle inward before they can rise.

Nietzsche's Aphorism (Paraphrased)

"You must become the one you are."

Interpretation:

Becoming is not a straight line. Nietzsche's vision is recursive—one must lose the path, discard borrowed guides, and spiral inward to become the thing already forming.

📖 Reflective Writing Prompts

- What objects or beliefs have you left behind recently?

- When has a path felt like repetition—but was actually transformation?

- What does the "center" of your spiral look like now?

⬜ Symbolic Inversion Challenge

Imagine the spiral collapses into a straight line.

- What do you lose? What do you gain?

- Create a symbol for "the shortest path that reveals the least."

🎨 Creative Drawing Prompt

Draw your personal spiral.

Place along it three objects you've discarded—and three you still carry.

Where are you now: on the edge, halfway, or almost at center?

Chapter 2: The Serpent's Gift

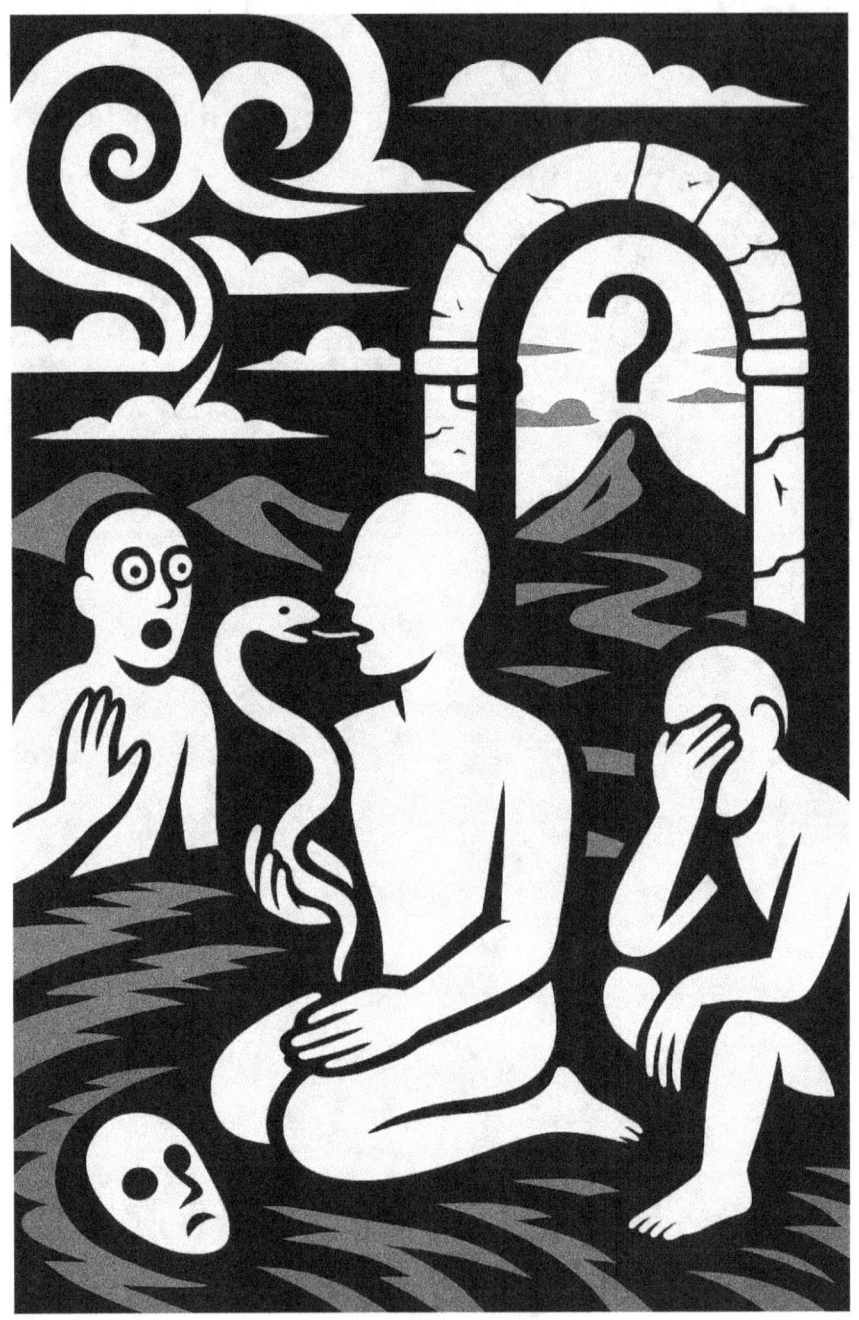

Image & Scene Summary

A central figure kneels with a serpent emerging from their mouth—not in fear, but as revelation.

Two onlookers: one stares wide-eyed, the other turns away.

Behind: a broken arch frames a mountain shaped like a question mark.

Above: clouds spiral, echoing the serpent's form.

◣ How It Works

Diagram Name: *Revelation Through Risk*

- Serpent = inner truth, dangerous knowledge, instinctual voice

- Mouth = release rather than repression

- Onlookers = reactions of the world: awe, fear, rejection

- Mountain/question mark = the new terrain that begins with a question
  Mechanism:

The truth within you may not be polite—it hisses, spirals, and shocks. To speak it is to lose comfort, but gain self.

Nietzsche's Aphorism (Paraphrased)

"The snake that cannot shed its skin must die."

Interpretation:

What emerges from within may frighten others—but to withhold it is to decay. Nietzsche reminds us: transformation is dangerous, and that is its power.

✏️ Reflective Writing Prompts

- What have you held inside that now demands release?

- Who in your life has responded with fear to your truth?

- What "question" is forming inside your mountain?

Symbolic Inversion Challenge

Imagine the serpent doesn't emerge—but coils inside silently.

- What does it become? What does it consume?

- Design a symbol for "the truth that devours from within."

🎨 Creative Drawing Prompt

Draw your own "serpent of speech."
Let it twist into words, shapes, or spirals—
whatever form your hidden truth takes when
released.

⬜⬜ Chapter 3: The Unasked Light

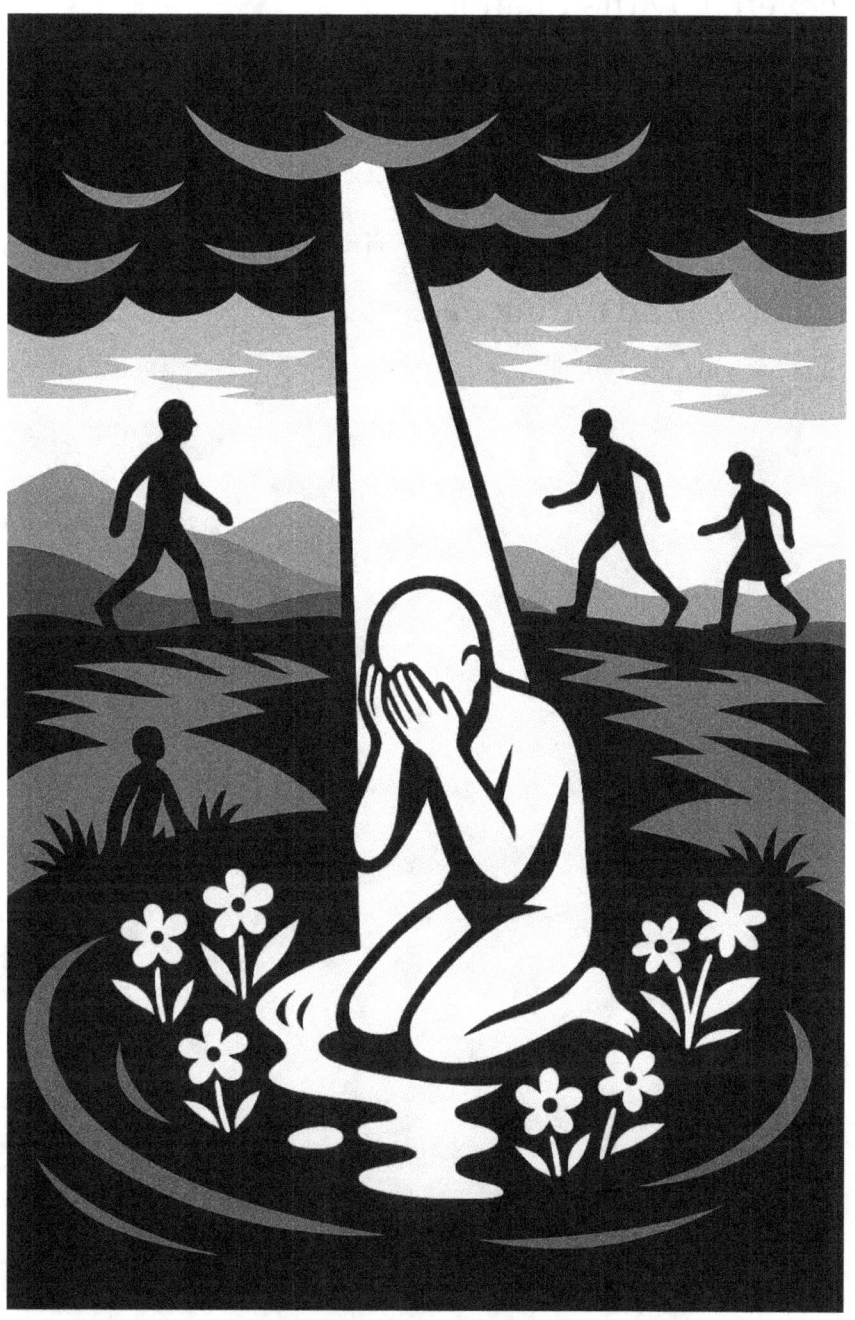

⬜ Image & Scene Summary

A shadowed figure kneels in a hollow, face covered by their hands.
 A single beam of light breaks through dark clouds above, touching them.
 Where the light lands, flowers begin to bloom.
 In the background, other figures pass by— unaware and untouched.

◣ How It Works

Diagram Name: *Light Without Petition*

- Hollow = despair, silence, withdrawal

- Light = grace, insight, or transformation—not earned, but encountered

- Flowers = unexpected growth triggered by vulnerability

- Others = those who move past pain without noticing its beauty
  Mechanism:

The most profound transformations are often not asked for—they arrive uninvited, and we are not always ready. But when they come, they bloom.

Nietzsche's Aphorism (Paraphrased)

"That which does not kill me makes me stronger."

Interpretation:

True strength is not willed—it is often revealed in collapse. The light appears not when called, but when needed. And not all are touched by it.

Reflective Writing Prompts

- When have you received something life-changing that you didn't ask for?

- What part of you grew from a moment of collapse?

- Are there flowers blooming in your life that others overlook?

⬡ Symbolic Inversion Challenge

Imagine the figure stands up and blocks the light.

- What stops blooming?

- Create a symbol for "the fear of receiving what heals."

🎨 Creative Drawing Prompt

Sketch a hollow.

Let the beam of light fall from an unexpected angle.

What begins to grow—and what still hides in shadow?

☐☐ Chapter 4: The Inner Dawn

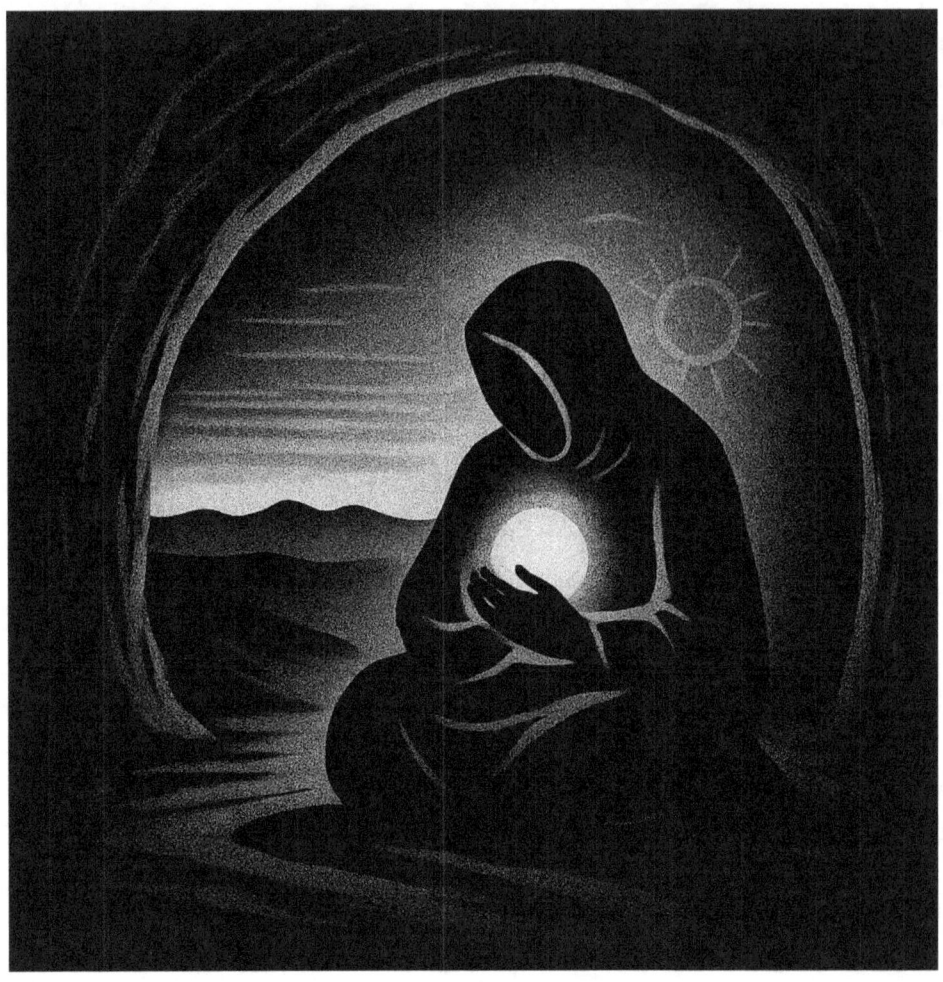

☐ Image & Scene Summary

A cloaked figure sits deep within a cave, hands cupped
over their chest as if guarding a flame.
 The walls of the cave glow faintly with a sun-like shape,
but the light clearly radiates from within the figure.
 Outside the cave: total darkness.
 Above the cave entrance: a distant line of mountaintops
just beginning to catch the early light.

◣ How It Works
Diagram Name: Light From Within

- Cave = introspection, withdrawal from external noise

- Inner flame = self-originated clarity, truth, or spirit

- Outer darkness = the absence of external validation or guidance

- Mountaintops = distant collective awakening, still faint
  Mechanism:

Nietzsche often rejected imposed light (religious, societal) in favor of an inner source. The dawn doesn't come from the sky—it comes from the self, slowly, quietly.

⬜ Nietzsche's Aphorism (Paraphrased)
"I love the man who justifies the future and redeems the past."
 Interpretation:
 The figure in the cave has stopped seeking from outside. They become the beginning of a new dawn—not by seeing it, but by being it.

Reflective Writing Prompts

- What inner truth do you protect that no one else sees yet?

- When have you chosen silence over applause?

- What part of your light has not yet risen into the world?

⬚ Symbolic Inversion Challenge
Imagine the cave is lit only from outside—and the figure carries nothing.

- What changes in the nature of the dawn?

- Design a symbol for "the light that disappears when watched."

🎨 Creative Drawing Prompt
Draw a figure in darkness—but glowing.
 Surround them with cave walls, silence, and one opening to the sky.
 Where does your figure's light come from?

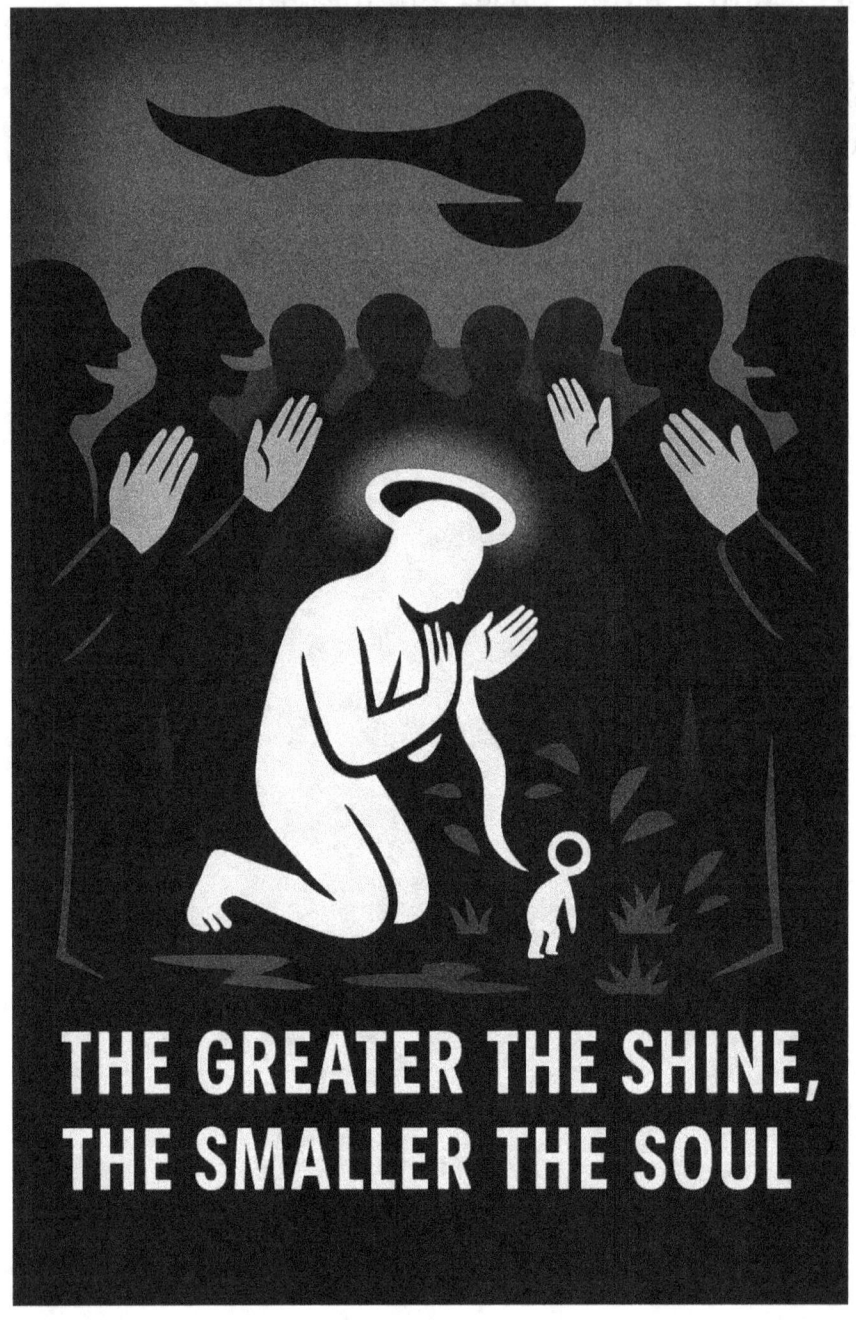

THE GREATER THE SHINE, THE SMALLER THE SOUL

⬚ Image & Scene Summary

A radiant figure kneels at the center of a crowd, surrounded by applause.

A halo glows above their head, and a stream of white light flows from their chest to a tiny, childlike figure below—fragile, silent.

Above, abstract forms float like fading masks or lips, symbols of muted voice.

The caption reads: "The greater the shine, the smaller the soul."

How It Works

Diagram Name: *Praise as Erosion*

- Halo = external virtue or the appearance of enlightenment

- Crowd = adoration, conformity, public validation

- Light stream = vitality leaking from self to symbol

- Child-soul = what remains of inward being— shrunken under the weight of performed perfection
  Mechanism:

Nietzsche warns that the crowd's applause often conceals decay. The more a person is praised for how they appear, the less room remains for who they are.

Nietzsche's Aphorism (Paraphrased)

"When virtue has a name, it ceases to be virtue."

 Interpretation:

 What glows may not grow. Praise too often rewards the costume of goodness, not the dangerous labor of truth. The soul that bends for applause forgets how to stand alone.

Reflective Writing Prompts

- When have you been praised in a way that made you feel smaller, not stronger?

- What part of you have you hidden to keep being applauded?

- What does the child beneath your shine still need?

Symbolic Inversion Challenge

Imagine the figure removes the halo and stands up—what happens to the crowd?

- What if the child-soul begins to grow?

- Create a symbol for "the quiet self returned through defiance."

🎨 Creative Drawing Prompt

Draw two versions of yourself: one radiant and admired, one smaller but free.
 Where does your soul feel safest—and where does it feel real?

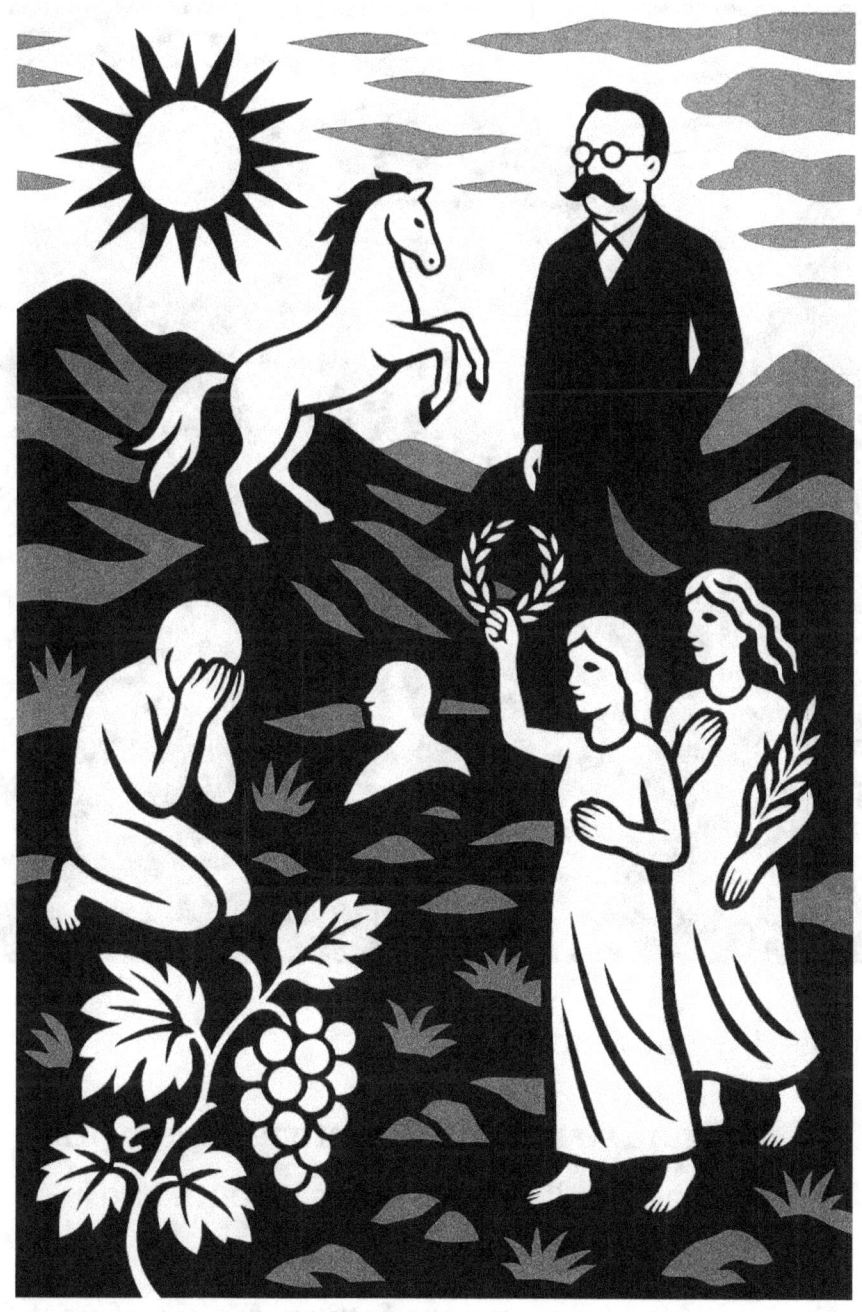

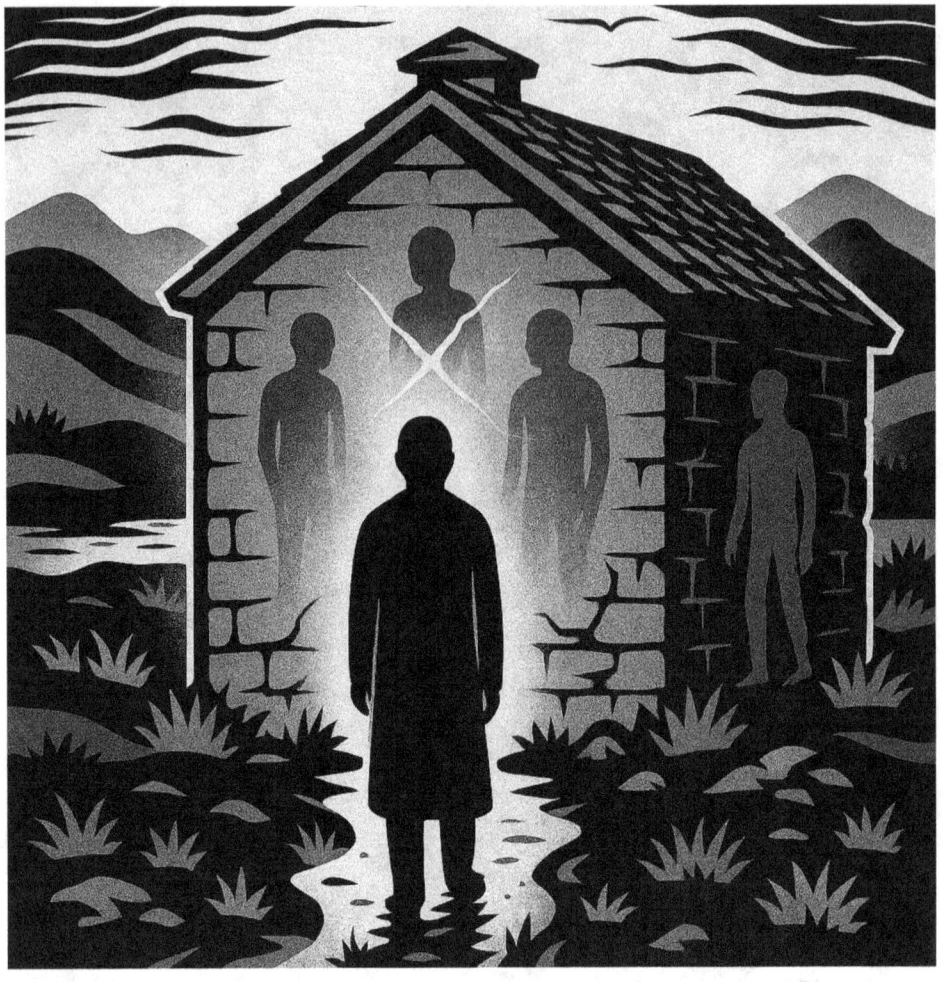

📖 Image & Scene Summary

A lone figure stands before a stone house with no doors or windows—its walls smooth and sealed.

Etched into the stone are fading images of past versions of the figure.

The house begins to crumble silently from within, as light seeps through forming cracks.

Behind the figure, the path they came from is nearly overgrown.

◣ How It Works

Diagram Name: *The Sealed Self and the Quiet Collapse*

- House = constructed self, protective identity, enclosure

- No doors = selfhood built without access—neither entry nor escape

- Fading versions = memory, repetition, ego

- Cracks = transformation beginning from within
  Mechanism:

When the self becomes architecture, it must eventually break. Nietzsche shows us that collapse is not failure—it is the first breath of a freer form.

Nietzsche's Aphorism (Paraphrased)

"You must be ready to burn yourself in your own flame. How could you rise anew if you have not first become ashes?"
Interpretation:
We build selves to survive—but survival isn't becoming. The sealed house is safety without breath. The crumbling is a gift.

Reflective Writing Prompts

- What "walls" have you built that no longer serve you?

- Which versions of yourself are still etched into your memory?

- What's beginning to crack open from the inside?

Symbolic Inversion Challenge

Imagine the house never cracks—but grows larger and stronger.

- What kind of life exists inside?

- Design a symbol for "the self that grows too safe to transform."

🎨 Creative Drawing Prompt

Draw your own "sealed house."

Add one crack, and choose what kind of light begins to emerge from it.

What's visible through that opening?

Chapter 8: Serpent, Fire, Hunger

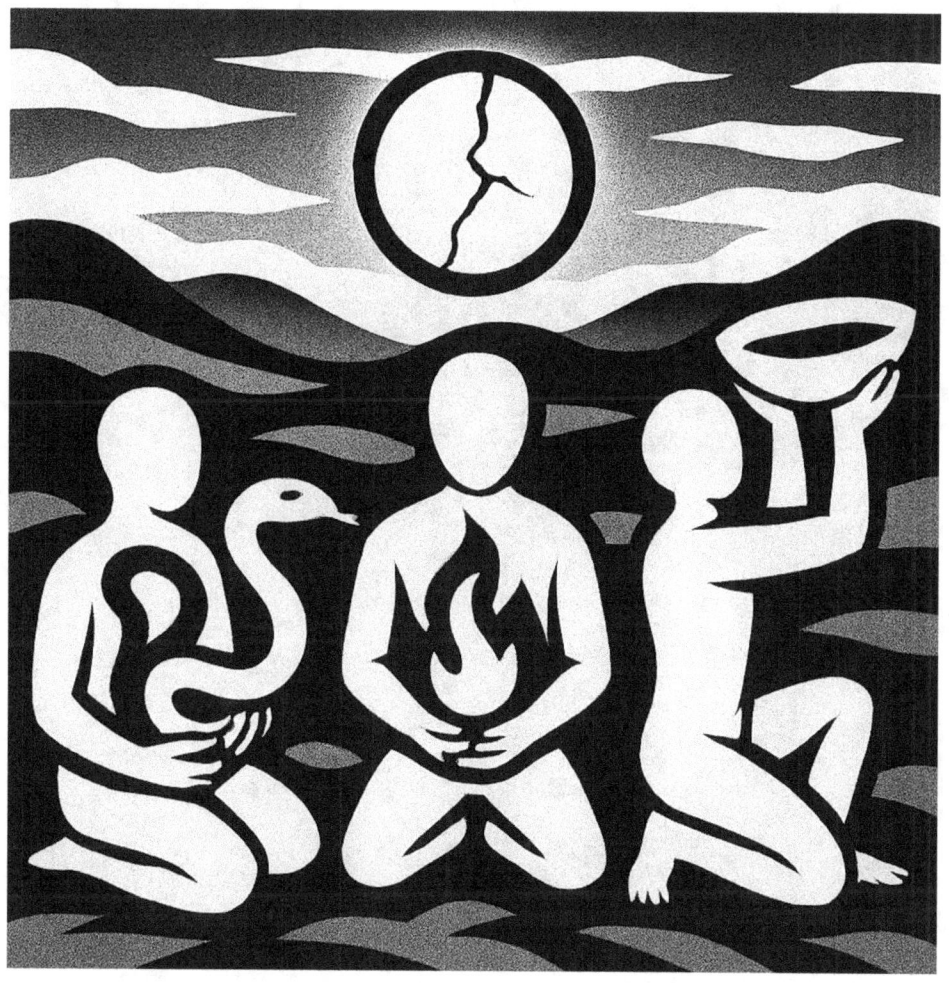

Image & Scene Summary

Three figures sit in a triangle.

One holds a coiled serpent.

One cradles a small flame.

One offers an empty bowl raised toward the sky.

None of them look at each other.

Above them floats a circular seal, cracked but unbroken.

◣ How It Works

Diagram Name: *The Triangle of Transformation*

- Serpent = instinct, danger, renewal

- Flame = creativity, destruction, rebirth

- Bowl = need, desire, vulnerability

- Seal = shared potential or order—fractured, but
  still whole
    Mechanism:

Each figure represents a part of being: primal
force, generative fire, and existential need.
Together they form a tense balance—one that
cannot heal unless they see each other.

Nietzsche's Aphorism (Paraphrased)

"Man is a rope stretched between beast and overman—a rope over an abyss."

Interpretation:

We are not one thing—we are pulled between instincts, longings, and creation. Nietzsche reminds us: harmony is not comfort, but the tension of becoming.

📖 Reflective Writing Prompts

- Which of the three symbols—serpent, fire, or bowl—feels most like you today?

- What happens in you when need, instinct, and creation are out of balance?

- What would it mean for the three figures to finally look at one another?

⬛ Symbolic Inversion Challenge

Imagine the seal above them shatters.

- What breaks loose—and what binds them afterward?

- Design a symbol for "unity through brokenness."

🎨 Creative Drawing Prompt

Sketch the triangle of serpent, fire, and hunger. Add a fourth object or figure that changes the balance.

What emerges from the new arrangement?

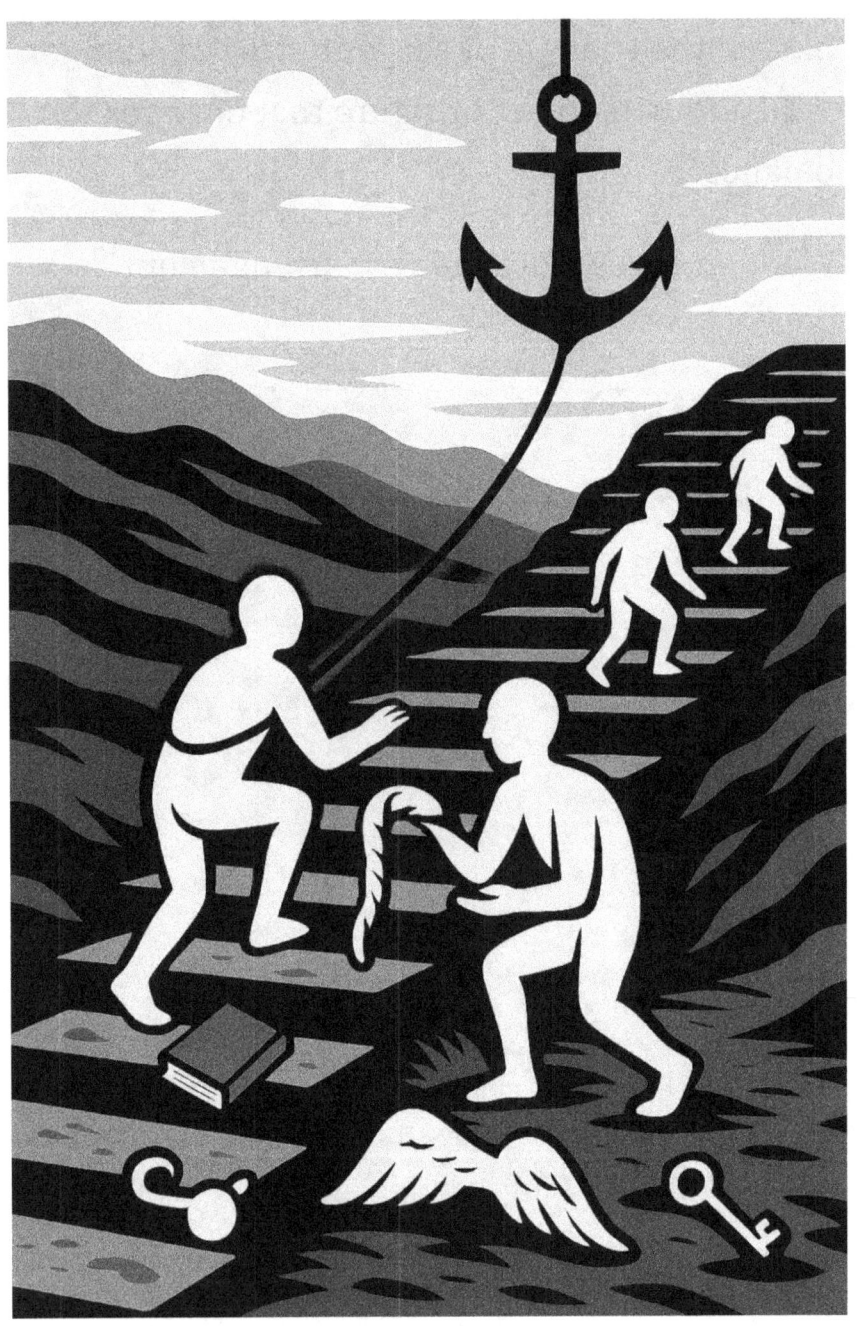

☐ Image & Scene Summary

A figure climbs a steep staircase carved into a mountainside.

 Above them floats a glowing anchor, weightless yet tethered to them by a rope.

 Other climbers ascend nearby—unburdened, unaware.

 Scattered on the steps below: an old book, a pair of wings, and a child's toy.

◣ How It Works

Diagram Name: *Burden Above, Not Below*

- Anchor = symbolic weight: belief, memory, identity

- Floating = paradox: heavy in meaning, but not physical

- Rope = invisible attachment, often chosen or inherited

- Discarded objects = past selves, forgotten tools, lost play
  Mechanism:

The greatest burdens aren't what drag us down—they're what hover above us, shaping how we move. Nietzsche's ascent is not blocked by failure, but by invisible loyalty.

Nietzsche's Aphorism (Paraphrased)

"One must still have chaos in oneself to give birth to a dancing star."

Interpretation:

What ties you to the floating weight above—duty, guilt, meaning—may not stop your climb, but it shapes how you climb. The anchor is not the past. It is your unfinished interpretation of it.

📖 Reflective Writing Prompts

- What belief or story still "floats above" you, quietly shaping your climb?

- Which of the discarded items on your path have you outgrown—and which might still be useful?

- Are you more afraid to cut the rope, or to reach the summit carrying it?

⬚ Symbolic Inversion Challenge

Imagine the anchor is lowered to the ground
and the climber lifts it.

- What happens next?

- Design a symbol for "a burden accepted instead of
  avoided."

🎨 Creative Drawing Prompt

Draw a figure climbing toward something both beautiful and heavy.

Where does your rope go—into the sky, into a memory, into a mirror?

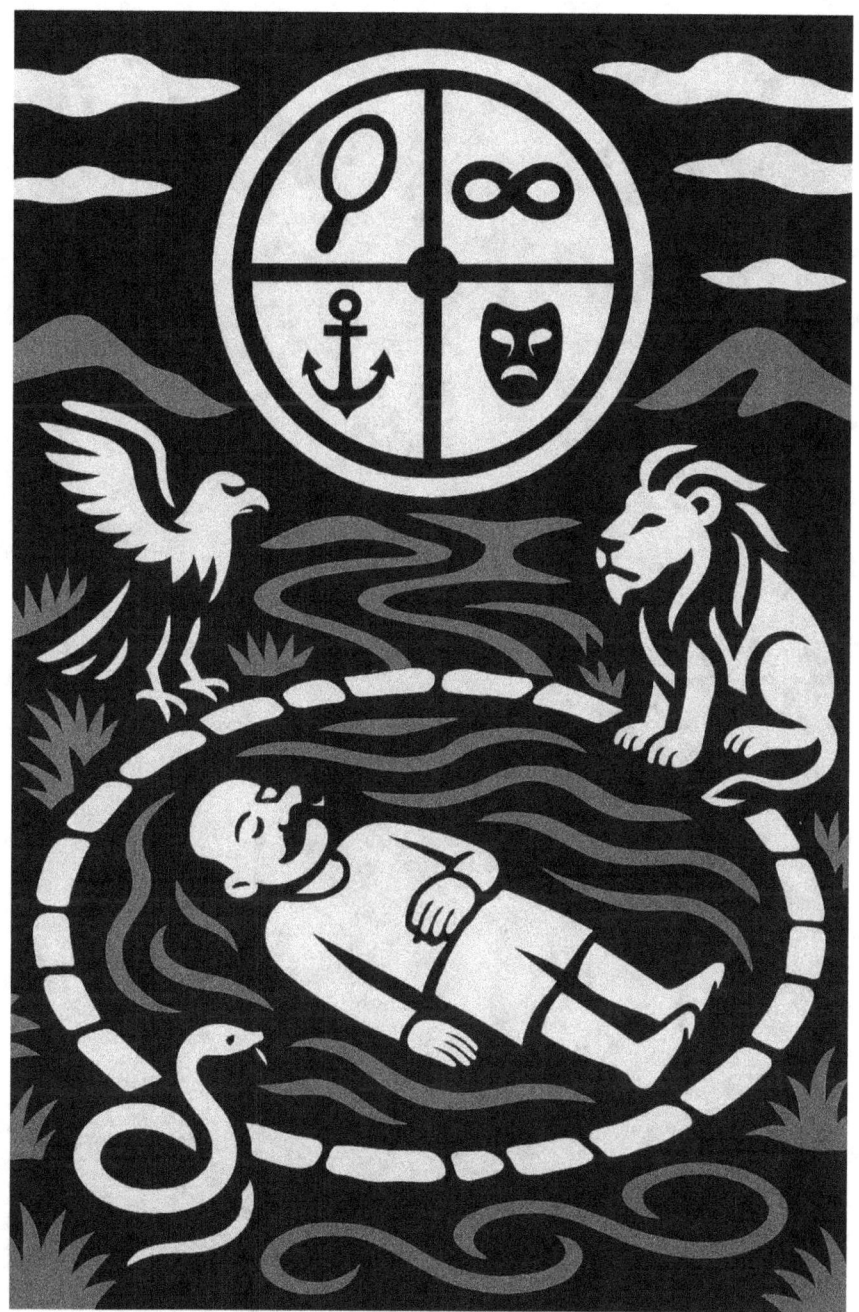

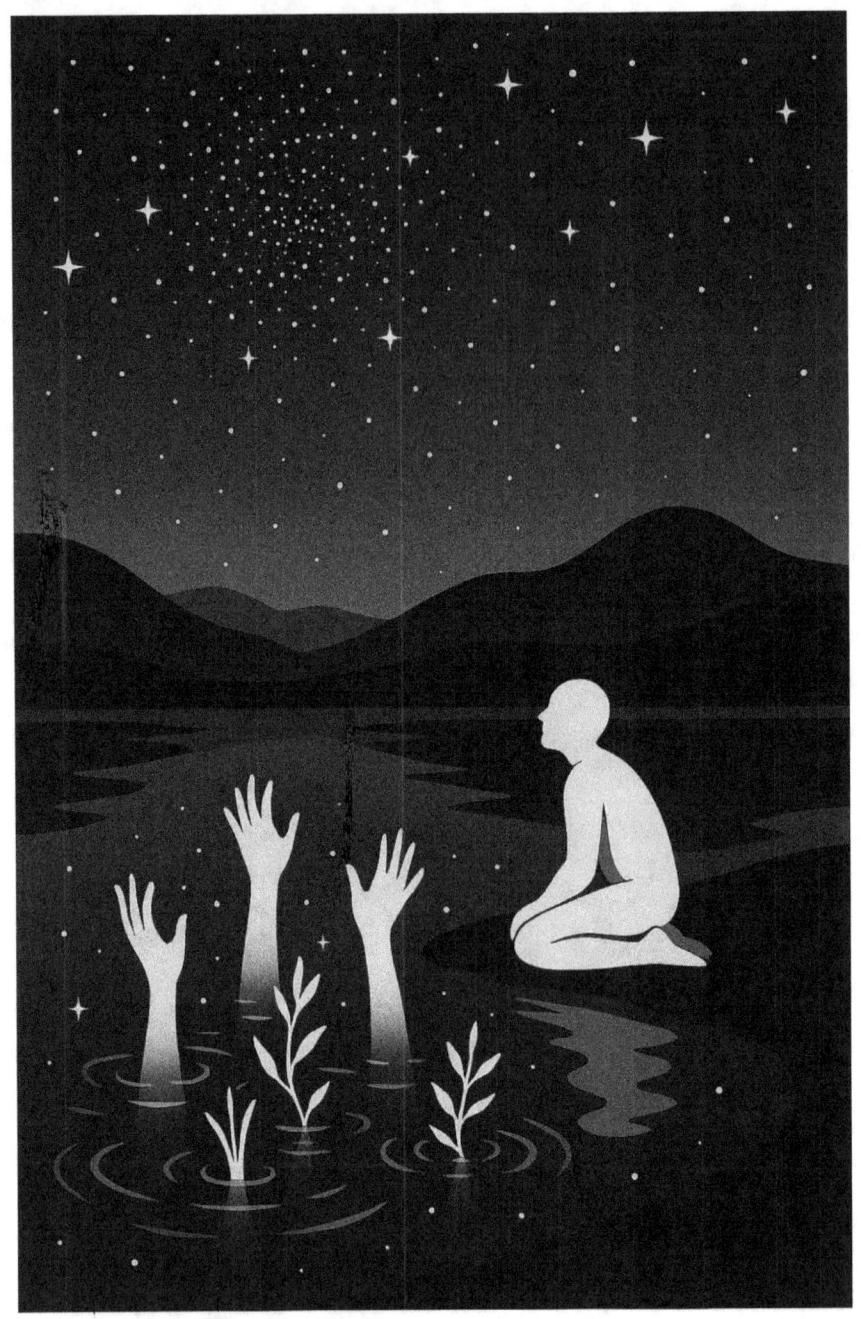

Chapter 10

⬜ Image & Scene Summary

A still lake reflects a brilliant star-filled sky.
From beneath the surface, delicate hands

reach upward—almost touching the stars, yet never breaking the water.

On the shore, a lone figure kneels, gazing at the stars, unaware of the reaching hands.

The stars swirl into a loose spiral, drawing the eye inward.

◣ How It Works

Diagram Name: *Reaching Without Arrival*

- Hands = yearning, memory, forgotten voices

- Water = surface of perception; beauty and illusion

- Stars = ideals, transcendence, unreachable light

- Spiral = slow return, unresolved longing
  Mechanism:

Nietzsche often wrote about desire unfulfilled—not as failure, but as creative tension. The image reminds us: the gap between longing and arrival may be the very space where meaning forms.

Nietzsche's Aphorism (Paraphrased)

"He who has a why to live can bear almost any how."

Interpretation:

The hands don't touch the stars—but they reach. The kneeling figure seeks above, unaware of what rises below. This is the Nietzschean dilemma: Do we aim upward, inward, or beneath?

✏️ Reflective Writing Prompts

- What are you reaching for that feels just out of reach?

- What have you ignored beneath your own reflection?

- Who or what in your life reaches toward you invisibly?

Symbolic Inversion Challenge

Imagine the stars fall into the lake—and the hands pull something out.

- What emerges?

- Create a symbol for "the unreachable that arrives in unexpected form."

🎨 Creative Drawing Prompt

Sketch a reflection that hides something reaching back.

What's beneath your stars?

Do your hands reach for light, for memory, or for something else entirely?

□□ Chapter 12: The Spiral Waltz

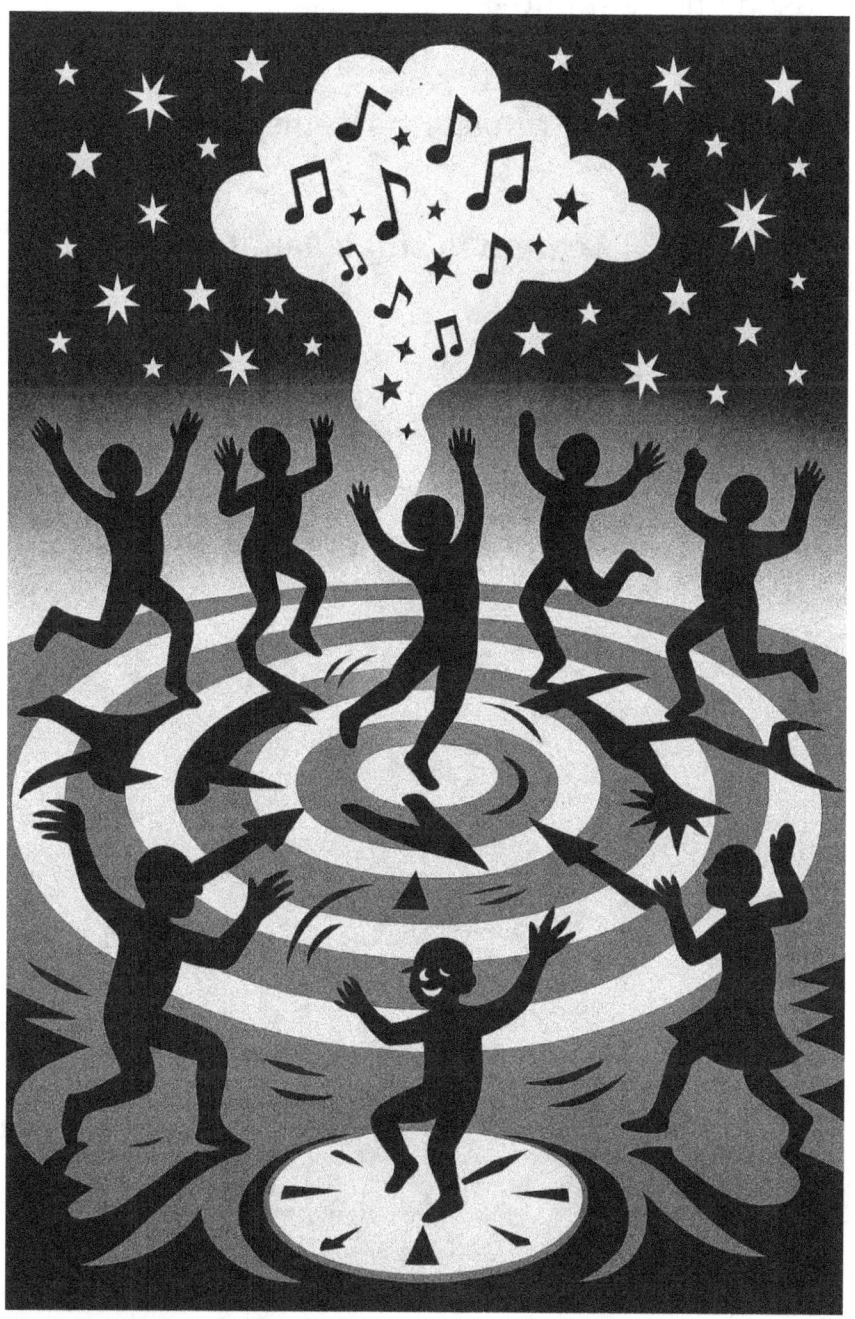

□ Image & Scene Summary

Silhouetted figures dance in a wide spiral, arms raised and feet mid-leap.

Their shadows form a clock face—but the hands point in strange, non-temporal directions.

At the spiral's center, a single laughing child spins alone.

Above them, a cloud bursts into tiny musical notes and stars.

◣ How It Works

Diagram Name: *Time Unwound Through Joy*

- Spiral dance = freedom in repetition, transformation through play

- Clock shadow = time made relative, repurposed into movement

- Child = renewal, innocence that knows and laughs

- Musical stars = joy as rhythm, not command
  Mechanism:

Nietzsche believed joy was revolutionary when it broke from duty. The spiral waltz is not escape from time—it's time danced into meaning.

☐ Nietzsche's Aphorism (Paraphrased)

"I would only believe in a god who could dance."

Interpretation:

This is not naivety—it is freedom born from struggle. The child at the center is not unaware; they are the only one who remembers that time, like sorrow, can be spun into music.

🖊️ Reflective Writing Prompts

- When have you felt the difference between structure and rhythm?

- What part of you still remembers how to dance without purpose?

- Is there a "clock" in your life that needs to be turned into a song?

◻ Symbolic Inversion Challenge

Imagine the dance stops—but the shadows keep spinning.

- What remains? What is lost?

- Create a symbol for "movement without joy."

🎨 Creative Drawing Prompt

Draw a spiral made of people or figures—but shaped like a clock.

Replace the numbers with symbols of rhythm or joy.

Who is at the center?

⬚ Chapter 13: The Laughing Ascent

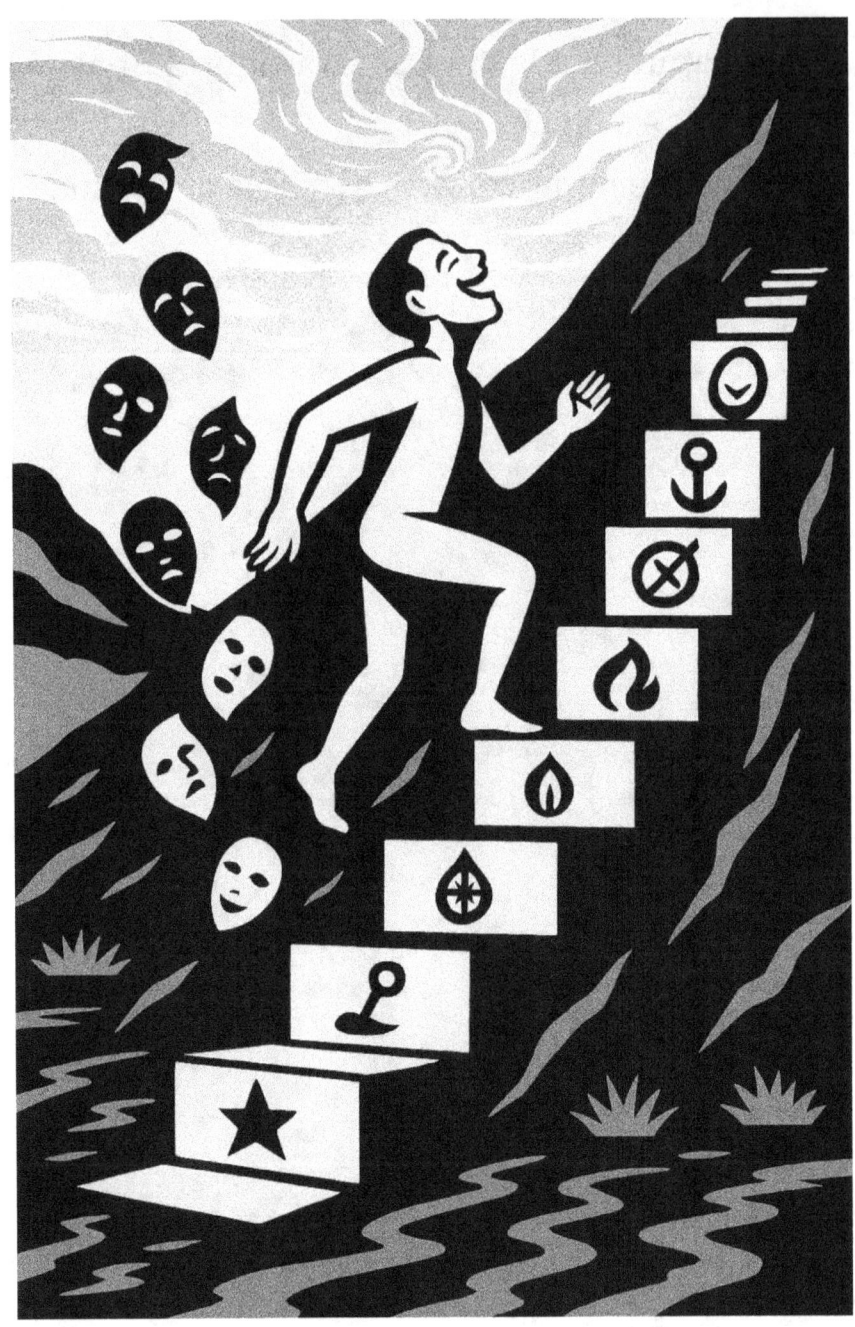

⬚ Image & Scene Summary

A lone figure climbs a winding mountain
staircase.

Each step bears a symbol: mirror, serpent, anchor, flame, wheel, mask, star.

Behind them, masks fall like leaves, drifting into the void.

Their face is tilted upward, mouth open in silent laughter.

At the summit: nothing but sky.

◣ How It Works

Diagram Name: *Ascent Through Shedding*

- Symbols = trials, truths, previous identities

- Masks = performed selves, outgrown illusions

- Laughter = joy not in victory, but in release

- Summit = not arrival, but openness
  Mechanism:

This is not a heroic climax—it is a joyful lightening. Nietzsche's laughter is not mockery. It is the release that comes when one has carried, confronted, and finally let go.

Nietzsche's Aphorism (Paraphrased)

"The higher we soar, the smaller we appear to those who cannot fly."

Interpretation:

True ascent is lonely—not because others fail to climb, but because the climber no longer needs to be seen. The laughter echoes because it no longer seeks reply.

Reflective Writing Prompts

- What symbols have shaped your path—and which ones have fallen away?

- What part of your past self have you finally outgrown?

- What does your laughter mean when no one else hears it?

⬜ Symbolic Inversion Challenge

Imagine the masks rise instead of fall,
returning to cling to the figure.

- What kind of ascent follows?

- Design a symbol for "the joy denied by unfinished
  shedding."

🎨 Creative Drawing Prompt

Sketch a staircase up a mountain.

Place a symbol on each step from your own journey.

At the top, leave it open—what does your sky look like?

⛰ Conclusion: The Joy That Follows the Shedding

The mountain has been climbed, not with conquest—but with laughter.
The masks have fallen. The rope has frayed.
The mirror has cracked, and still it reflects the stars.

This book was not about reaching a summit.
It was about leaving behind what cannot ascend—
the false halo, the sealed house, the roles inherited rather than chosen.

Each symbol encountered was not a truth to believe,
but a weight to be carried until it could be set down.
And in that release, Zarathustra smiled.

So ask yourself:

- Did you speak the serpent's truth?

- Did you become the cave's light?

- Did you laugh, not because it was easy—but because it was free?

☐ Coming in Book IV

Book IV begins not at the top of the mountain, but beyond it.

Zarathustra no longer climbs.
 He listens.
 He watches.
 He follows stars that will not stay still.

In the final volume:

- Prophecy gives way to pause.

- Laughter fades into quiet rupture.

- The symbols themselves rebel.

> What happens when even joy must be overcome?
> Who speaks when Zarathustra goes silent?

The final silence is not the end.
 It is the invitation to begin again.

📖 Glossary of Symbols and Ideas

Spiral

A path that circles inward—not toward confusion, but toward depth. In Nietzschean thought, the spiral represents return with transformation: the eternal recurrence of experience, but re-approached with new will.

Serpent

A recurring symbol of instinct, wisdom, and danger. In Book III, the serpent emerges as speech—a truth that must be released, not repressed.

Light (Inner)

Unlike divine light from above, this light arises from within—a glow born of suffering, silence, and becoming. It cannot be given, only uncovered.

The Anchor

Typically a symbol of grounding, here it floats—revealing how some attachments weigh not through gravity, but through memory, guilt, or unexamined loyalty.

The Halo

A glow of perceived virtue or recognition. When sought too eagerly, it grows brighter while the self shrinks into nothingness.

The Sealed House

A constructed identity so complete it has no entry or exit. Over time, it collapses from within, revealing that the only true escape is self-created rupture.

Flame

The small fire held gently represents creative force, fragile and sacred. It is both danger and offering.

Empty Bowl

Symbol of desire, hunger, and openness—but also vulnerability. Held upward, it asks: not for power, but for something new to enter.

Clock / Time

In Book III, time is not a tyrant but a dance floor. Spirals and shadows form clocks that measure not seconds, but directions.

The Laughing Ascent

The final act of joyful detachment. Laughter not from conquest—but from release. It is the sound made when nothing more needs to be said or held.

Mask

Repeated from earlier books. In Book III, masks fall not in defiance—but as byproducts of ascent. They are not thrown off—they are shed.

Child (at the center)

A return to innocence—but one that now includes memory, sorrow, and strength. The child in Book III is not naïve. It is the last form of wisdom.

www.ingramcontent.com/pod-product-compliance
Lightning Source LLC
Chambersburg PA
CBHW081610220526
45468CB00010B/2827